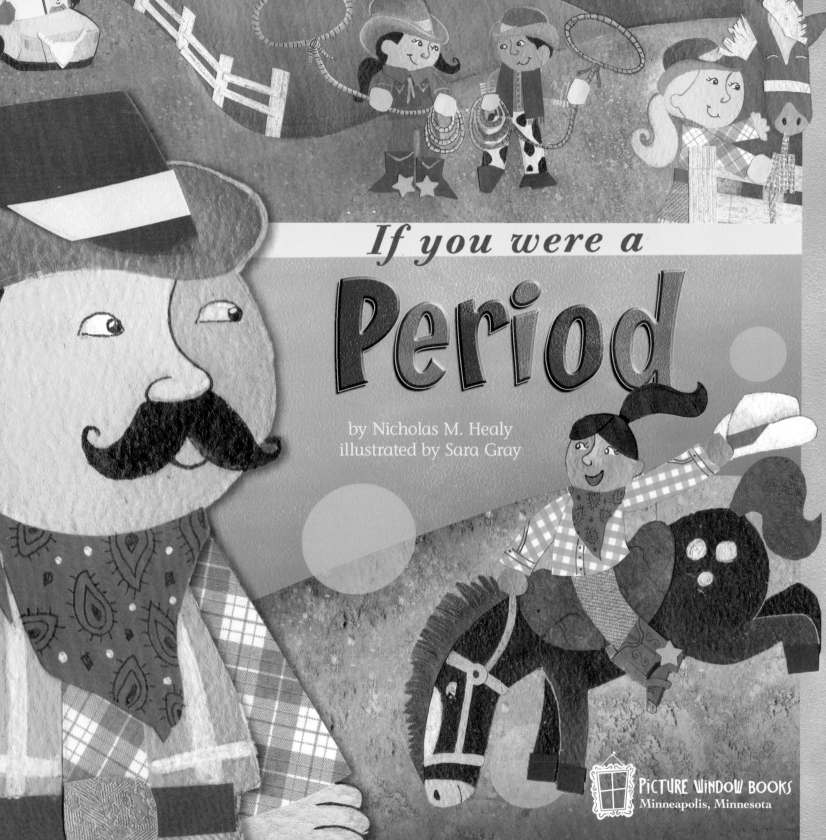

If you were a

Period

by Nicholas M. Healy
illustrated by Sara Gray

period (○) a punctuation mark used at the end of most sentences and abbreviations

PICTURE WINDOW BOOKS
Minneapolis, Minnesota

Editor: Jill Kalz
Designer: Tracy Davies
Page Production: Melissa Kes
Art Director: Nathan Gassman
The illustrations in this book were created with acrylics.

Picture Window Books
151 Good Counsel Drive
P.O. Box 669
Mankato, MN 56002-0669
877-845-8392
www.picturewindowbooks.com

Printed in the United States of America.

Library of Congress Cataloging-in-Publication Data
Healy, Nick.
If you were a period / by Nicholas M. Healy ;
illustrated by Sara Gray.
p. cm. — (Word Fun)
Includes index.
ISBN 978-1-4048-5332-4 (library binding)
ISBN 978-1-4048-5333-1 (paperback)
1. English language—Punctuation—Juvenile literature.
2. School—Juvenile literature. 3. Language arts (Primary)
I. Gray, Sara, ill. II. Title.
PE1450.H355 2009
428.2—dc22
                    2008039314

Looking for periods?
Watch for the BIG marks throughout the book.

Special thanks to our advisers for their expertise:

Rosemary G. Palmer, Ph.D., Department of Literacy
College of Education, Boise State University

Terry Flaherty, Ph.D., Professor of English
Minnesota State University, Mankato

... you would be last in line.

Harry and Erin run to the bus stop.

4

School starts today.

If you were a period, you would mark the end of a sentence.

Harry likes to ride up front.
Erin sits beside him.

6

Off they go to Cowpoke Elementary School.

If you were a period, you would bring a sentence to a stop. Some people might even call you a "full stop."

Lots of kids go to Cowpoke Elementary.

Some kids walk to school.

8

Some kids ride the bus.

Some kids ride horses.

9

If you were a period, you would be used in shortened words, called abbreviations. You could shorten, or abbreviate, an address.

The street Billy lives on is called Bonney St.

The road Butch lives on is called Sundance Rd.

The drive Erin lives on is called Cody Dr.

If you were a period, you would shorten the titles used before people's names. For example, you would shorten *mister* and *missus*.

Mr. James' Classroom

Mr. James teaches second grade.

Mrs. Starr's Classroom

Mrs. Starr teaches kindergarten.

12

If you were a period, you would also come after initials.

The physical education class is called P.E.

CORRAL

13

If you were a period, you could shorten a date.

Mr. James reminds the kids that it's Tuesday. He says it's the fifth day of September.

RODeo Times

Tues., Sept. 5

Roping Contest

If you were a period, you could help make a list of numbered items.

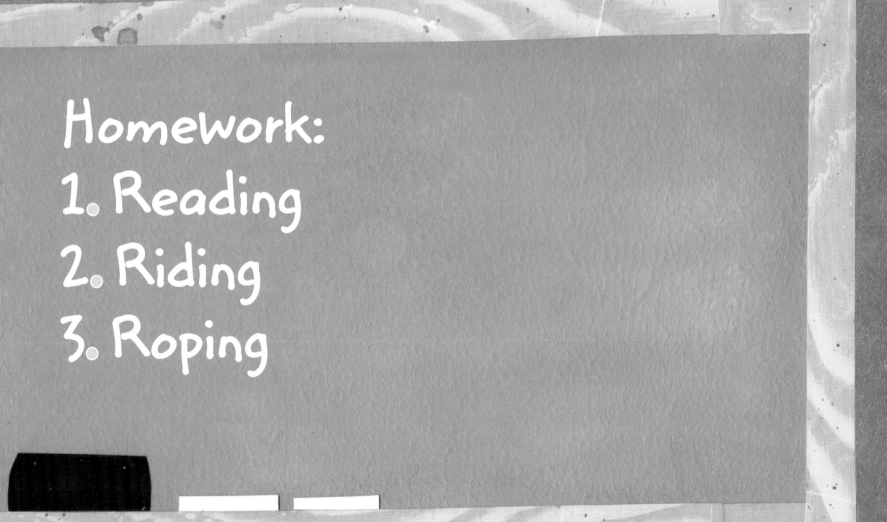

Homework:
1. Reading
2. Riding
3. Roping

If you were a period, you would help tell time. You would show whether the time is morning or afternoon.

Harry's class learns to lasso at 10 a.m.

16

All of the kids eat their vittles at 11:30 a.m.

At 1 p.m., Erin's class sings cowboy songs.

17

If you were a period, you would not ask a question.

What do we say when we want a horse to stop?

18

If you were a period, you would not exclaim anything.

Whoa!

If you were a period, you would declare something. You would make a statement.

That is right.

19

If you were a period, you would have the answers.

Before the final bell rings, Harry's teacher asks, "Do we use a period when asking a question?"
The second-graders shout, "No!"
The teacher says, "That is right."

On the way home, Erin asks, "What does a period do?"
Harry says, "It tells a sentence 'Whoa!'"
Erin says, "Oh, that's easy."

21

You would bring things to a stop ...

...if you were a period.

Quick Review

Periods are used at the end of declarative sentences. These sentences make a statement. They are not questions or exclamations.

> The kids love Cowpoke Elementary○
> Their school is cool○

Periods are used after abbreviations.

> The winter break begins Dec○ 20 and ends Jan○ 2.

A period comes after someone's title but before his or her name.

> Dr○ John Holliday helps when kids get sick or hurt.

Periods help us tell time.

> Harry wakes up at 6 a○m○ and goes to bed at 8 p○m○

A period can be used after initials.

> Christopher Bartholomew Jones likes to be called C○ B○ Jones.

Fun with Periods

Periods have an important job to do at the end of sentences. But they get used in other ways, too. One sentence can have lots of periods. For example:

> After Principal Patrick F. Garrett rings the bell at 8 a.m., he looks out of his office window and watches the P.E. classes on the playground.

On a scrap of paper, write a sentence that includes at least four periods. Can you fit even more into one sentence?

23

Glossary

abbreviation—one or more letters that stand for a longer word

a.m.—an abbreviation for the time between midnight and noon

declarative sentence—a sentence that makes a statement, or makes something known

exclaim—to say something loudly or with excitement

full stop—another name for a period, most often used in Great Britain and Canada

initial—the first letter of a name or word

period—a punctuation mark used at the end of most sentences and abbreviations

p.m.—an abbreviation for the time between noon and midnight

punctuation—marks used to make written language clear

title—a word or group of words used to show a person's position or job

Index

To Learn More

More Books to Read

Heinrichs, Ann. *Punctuation*. Chanhassen, Minn.: Child's World, 2006.

Pulver, Robin. *Punctuation Takes a Vacation*. New York: Holiday House, 2003.

Salzmann, Mary Elizabeth. *Period*. Edina, Minn.: ABDO Publishing Company, 2001.

On the Web

FactHound offers a safe, fun way to find educator-approved Internet sites related to this book.

Here's what you do:
1. Visit www.facthound.com
2. Choose your grade level.
3. Begin your search.

This book's ID number is 9781404853324

Look for all of the books in the Word Fun: Punctuation series:

If You Were a Comma
If You Were a Period
If You Were a Question Mark
If You Were an Apostrophe
If You Were an Exclamation Point
If You Were Quotation Marks

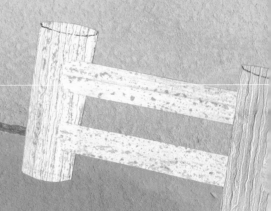